神的愛很忙

God's Love Is Very Busy
© David Seung and Cathexis Northwest Press

No part of this book may be reproduced without written permission of the publisher or author, except in reviews and articles.

First Printing: 2019

Paperback ISBN: 978-1-7330279-4-6

Cover art by C. M. Tollefson
Designed and edited by C. M. Tollefson

Cathexis Northwest Press

cathexisnorthwestpress.com

神 God's
的 Love
愛 Is
很 Very
忙 Busy

By David Seung

Cathexis Northwest Press

神的愛很忙	9
Oolong	10
火病	11
Big Meal on the Last Day	12
Clean Break	13
We Are Both Alone Again	14
Expecting	15
アメリカン・ドリーム	16
부대찌개	17
Quiet Life in a Wooded Glen (王蒙, Yuan Dynasty)	18
I Learned 仁 From Confucius	19
Man, Now	20
The Butcher Returned in Clean Clothes	21
The Architecture of a Soundless Begging	22
The Old Man's Closet	23
The Gorge Burned Because Boys Played With Firecrackers	24
Hemophiliac	25
Odio	26
남자 아이	27
Bitter Chomp	28
I Look Nothing Like My Mother	29
He Waved and i could taste those Fingers	30
画家剪头发	31

神的愛很忙

The oldest child wets
envelope edges with broad, firm licks,
steps over the facedown father,
impregnates the mailbox.

Oolong

Tea leaves bleed the color of sick faces
in otherwise pure water –
its surface plays with sunlight like a moon's wink

my teacup punctures the table's blank balance –
memories steep in silence –
the chessboard waits without adversary

mellow fragrance swells like young pride, pregnant
with sky and astringent earth,
rapidly aging as all small creatures.

On the counter: fresh chive blossoms, ginger –
I still cook with full flavor
As if to prove a point

while this ripe sun decays I will toast spices
fry lamb strips like autumn leaves
bless the air with popping fat and pepper

I will blister chilies, slice
scallions for my own tastes only –
slurp your thickened ghosts without audience.

Steam has stopped rising from my tea –
I drink in warm gulps, thinking of the present –
its taste has grown bitter.

火病

yawning mug inhales black coffee, sweetened by foaming cloudlight
sky's thin whites set overhead, the pale sun a poached yolk
I eat a noon breakfast, with no one to wake for.

Big Meal on the Last Day

The pork belly sky sat
Rendering fat layers of light
That popped, dripped,
Burned lightly by surprise.

The grease of the evening seemed infinite
Like we could watch the sun dying forever.

Clean Break

He Left

dew on steering wheel
knuckles crack white in cold air
silence begets tears

She Left

dirt in fingernails
laying down infant gardens
fed by the old rot

my mother was born
between perforated grins
now torn from their mouths

We Are Both Alone Again

Bald moon reflects off old rivers
streetlamps torch newborn streams
on wet roads, windows of closed
dark markets, a face
I can neither dry nor discern

Expecting

Nightly as I walk beneath full autumn,
the moonstain soaked through ash clouds
like cigarette burns,
the hook-fingered birch in colorless decay

I watch the days leave lesser traces,
waiting for that naked infant
Winter to come shrieking into
a world bored of dry comforts

アメリカン・ドリーム

living room flames dance –
sheltered pleasure paid in chopped
wood like Baptist heads

window burps warm glow –
I crunch frost with heavy steps –
breath twirls by streetlights

부대찌개

young spiders threw threads to catch wind
and got caught by whims of a typhoon –
boys were shipped to battlefields
towns were stripped of clothes
girls were milked for morale
by occupying saviors
who came to stroke the clashing waves
of fraternal blood

like dogs lap puddles poured by storms
women filled their pots with leftover rations
and children ate military stew
which wasn't all that different from the old jjigae

Quiet Life in a Wooded Glen (王蒙, Yuan Dynasty)

pull me from a womb
wrapped taught with tasseled trees;
rocks cradle the cry
of quiet waiting

bring me out from
the staining of autumn,
pain of home falling
blush of plum
blossoms beneath a white sky -
bent low to kiss the hands of high reaching mountains,
grasping at heaven
and the promise of orchids

tear me from right angles
straight lines
ink trails like veins
jagged stretch of cliffs
staggered breath of wildness
slow peel of vapor
off morning leaves
pulse of peaceful earth

I am from the birth
of old bones and beards -
where tall notes of a zither
join the resting wind.

I Learned 仁 From Confucius

The Himba people in Namibia have no word for blue
they draw no distinction between distant hues
of sky and canopy

I look up
beneath the two bent strokes of 人 (rén)
pulled apart by ham-handed men and thin-fingered painters
as a whishbone, greasy and not meatless.
I see the word
MAN smeared
across a B-29's reflective chassis,
across open-mouthed attacks of tongue and tight hands,
across a woman's dark bruises,
and I see it painted
on fermenting jars of virtue
on fathers strumming minor-keyed songs with low voices,
on small envelopes of cash crossing borders

and from the soil of boyhood
we look up to men
and are given no word of distinction

Man, Now

Before us there was coal
coal in the holes they carved through mountains
coal in the black breath of smokestacks rising
coal, dark in the pooling pupils of men who outworked the sun

and before them was war
war that made men heroes
war that made men broken
war that makes scarred hands shake and teaches pain in different languages

and we know only to broaden our shoulders,
paint our blank banners any colors we like,
draw lines between muscles we raise like children.
we have not sweat blood
we have not washed our hands and hair in it
we have forgotten our fathers' hatred and learned to speak our own

no tall officer put me on a bus with a bayonet
I never had to steal food to feed others
I have time even
to waste like this.

The Butcher Returned in Clean Clothes

The butcher's son learned how God
makes a man
from cleaning pigs
"They've got pretty much all the same parts"
his father told him, finger through an aorta
as a puppet spine.

On the day he left
his clothes were clean
and when he came back
they reeked of soap.

"How many Germans did ya kill?"

The boy got up from the smack
with lingering skull-throb, mouth
caught on shock like a hooked fish

the butcher aimed a thick finger at his
flesh and blood, dry-eyed, jowl in tight reflex,
said "don't you say anything like that again."

I have inherited both these faces.

The Architecture of a Soundless Begging

Plexiglass doors sigh
gray specked breath –
parking lot exhaust, cigarettes,
false sunshine of fried chicken grease

the building is damp with dull blue
of morning, we get to work
correcting dimness
with soft buzzing fluorescents

the steady drip of Folgers is an incense pendulum

my brother shucks plastic clamshells
for donut holes, we arrange
quartered Costco muffins
in skin-tone mosaics

this church was once a family
fun center. The Spirit
fills the space
built for a jungle gym

a Yamaha keyboard is a pipe organ

the untrimmed pastor
in cargo shorts and Keens
consecrates a cup
of Welch's, shed for us

my brother colors Bible scenes with bright non-toxics
my father prays, packing a pistol
my grandpa says he hasn't had a drink in years,
he is here to prove something to my mother, who forgives him daily

his glasses are stained windows

The Old Man's Closet

Streetlamps cast shadows in daylight –
an old gun in a box beneath his unworn ties

Our fathers taught us pain in different languages
tongues death-stiffened, unstilled
rattling in their cages
our mothers patched holes in our jeans
with uniform scraps
the off-color tickled our unhairy knees

Grapefruits seemed bitter once
as black coffee
but we grew into bitterness like hand-me-down pants
stopped putting sugar in our oats
stirred ourselves into unsweetened mornings

The Gorge Burned Because Boys Played With Firecrackers

Rainfall tore down the veil of smoke
Like a falling body clutching a shower curtain
and the city
naked, wet, ungendered
exhaled the gray petrichor of asphalt.

The space between rooftops and gunky white
sky a scrotum after a cold wash

there was something motherly, too
about the forested hills
that justified, gave form
to the careless passage of an opaque river

Hemophiliac

Night skin light-blemished
star-freckled
moon-scarred, cut –
white blood leaking from a wound
that won't stay shut

wolf-moan of sirens
that hunt behind blocks
of buildings we built to blot the blood sky,
clot the unspoken closeness of death

Odio

the faces that surrounded me grew cold   while I was cold no matter what I wore
my eyes burned holes through every laugh I sold   I tried to burn the meat off of my core
I drowned in all the ugliness I'd drink   my own reflection drowned me in the sink
          all in the time it took the moon to wink
I couldn't break the chrysalis of noise   my eyes grew mute and images grew loud
I never felt a penetrating voice   the winter sun sat shy behind the clouds
since no one took the time to look within   my skeleton stood bold behind my skin
          all in the time it took the sky to spin
though no one tried to crack my casket mood   though everyone stared cruelly at my corpse
though nothing ugly worked to mask its truth   though everything I saw was cruelly warped
though nowhere offered up an honest calm   though everywhere demanded all my calm
          the moon still bats her cat eye at my palms –
          the quiet came to wash me in the night
          the darkness let me savor every light

남자 아이

straw's mosquito penetration, vacuum cheeks inhale
wash of medicine sweetness, wet cold flushes arid ribs
rapid tax of gaunt droplets – sound of juicebox implosion

Bitter Chomp

I gnashed wet flesh
with a closed throat
held skeletal pith and sinewy threads
in a closed mouth
strained sticky sweet blood
through my clenched teeth
        spat

the fat splash joined the gray current –
rainwater in a gutter
cigarette riverstones –
swallowed by a stormdrain
who chugged dryly through iron teeth,
wet decay of greenless leaves

I was left with only skin –
bodiless, bitter
broken into brief pieces
goosebumped as a girl's leg
glinting with carnauba wax –
that left a chalky buzz on the teeth
that pierced it

I ate orange peels and pith
to feel matter interject
my stomach's vain clawing –
cast stones into the acid tide

I Look Nothing Like My Mother

We watched Beauty through zooglass
computers. Our own waxing cheeks
waning eyes the backwash of unlit screens

America is called 美国 (beautiful country) –
pubes dyed blond –
I didn't know what "double eyelids" were until

my aunt came home, her own
pulled up like skirts afraid of pupils' mud,
eyes unsqueezed by a smile's press.

My White Mother
whom I have always failed to resemble
said I could benefit from the same

surgery. Having robbed my Mother of a Child
in her image, a reflection of flesh and face,
I considered propping my eyes wide, cropping my nose

scrubbing my cheeks gaunt until
I could tell you I was her son
and you wouldn't laugh.

He Waved and i could taste those Fingers

Hands the red leather of a shedding oak
broken love-lines and cracked white
callouses like dog froth

Hands that Held me down to a dorm floor
Drowned me in damp heat of wolf-tongued flesh
Found my skin where i tried to hide it

Hands that Ran rabid with spiders' legs
Spun my body in a fetal curl
Spread it like a broken yolk

Hands that forgot they were hands
Hands i am trying to forgive
but cannot touch

Hands smaller than my own. i could have
beaten him up. they all Laughed when i told them
He Laughed the whole time

and i can only laugh back or be Laughed at
smack my mind when it comes to confide
crack my eyes like white peppercorns.

i saw those Hands Waving at my dinner table
Wiping color and sound from ham-sweet air
and we all waved back, Chewing.

画家剪头发

春花落上土
晓雨冷强奸
鸟不思夜风
你自画像不美

Artist Cuts Her Hair

Spring blossoms fall broken on soil
morning rain's cold rape
birds forget last night's wind
your self-portraits are not beautiful

Cathexis Northwest Press

www.ingramcontent.com/pod-product-compliance
Lightning Source LLC
Chambersburg PA
CBHW051354070526
44584CB00025B/3764